My ENEMY
My FRIEND

SECOND EDITION

a story of reconciliation from the
VIETNAM WAR

Brigadier General Dan Cherry, USAF, (Ret.)

with
Fran Erickson

ISBN 978-0-692-00007-6
Printed in Canada

Library of Congress Control Number: 2008911642

Published by Aviation Heritage Park Inc.
P.O. Box 1526
Bowling Green, KY 42102-1526
(270) 779-4186
www.aviationheritagepark.com

Aviation Heritage Park is a 501 (c)3 charitable nonprofit organization.
Proceeds from the sale of this book will go to the Aviation Heritage
Park perpetual maintenance fund to protect and maintain historic aviation artifacts.

Book design by Katie Clark
Photography by John Fleck
Cover art by Maxine McCaffrey, courtesy Air Force Art Collection
Aircraft illustrations by Jack Morris, JDMC Aviation Graphics
Portrait of Hong My by Allen Polt
"The MiG That Didn't Get Away" painting by Lou Drendel

Dedicated to
MY DAUGHTERS & GRANDDAUGHTERS

Jill & Kim
Maggie, Maddie, Amelia & Claire

The lights of my life

ACKNOWLEDGEMENTS

One thing I know for certain is that any complex and worthwhile endeavor is never accomplished alone. So many people have advised and assisted me with this project I could never begin to thank them all adequately. To all who helped, thank you.

If this book has any merit and is enjoyed by its readers it is only because of the word magic performed by an extraordinary lady, Fran Erickson. Her total command of the English language transformed my jumble of words into something much more respectable. It wouldn't have happened without you, Frannie.

And to John Fleck my heartfelt gratitude for your friendship and your exceptional photography. John, your pictures alone tell this story.

Katie Clark of Western Kentucky University also deserves special recognition. Katie's creativity and sense of style melded together words, graphics and pictures in a way that makes the story come alive. Thanks, Katie.

My sincere thanks also to the Aviation Heritage Park Board of Directors. Their unwavering dedication and commitment to this project have taken a dream and made it a reality in a very short period of time. Our community is better because of your efforts and I am very proud to call all of you friends.

To all Vietnam veterans, wherever you may be, thank you for your sacrifice and service.

And to Syl, my one true love. Thanks for hanging in there with me through it all.

Dan Cherry

*This book made possible
by the generous support of our sponsors:*

JOHN & PEGGY HOLLAND

ENGLISH, LUCAS, PRIEST AND OWSLEY, LLP

BOB & NORMA JEAN KIRBY AND FAMILY

BARBARA STEWART

DON & LINDA VITALE

And special thanks to:

Larry Bailey
Bowling Green Area Convention & Visitors Bureau
Katie Clark
Lou Drendel
Fred & Fran Erickson
Ed Faye
John Fleck
Margo Grace of Friesens Printing
Jack Morris
Hong & Lan Nguyen
Thu Uyen Nguyen-Pham
Bob and Carolyn Pitchford
Allen Polt
The Thundergeezers
Pat Trenner
The Walking Group
Hank Wohltjen

CONTENTS

INTRODUCTION

Bowling Green, Kentucky is a great town—just the right size to find what you need without fighting the hassles of big city life. But it's the people—special people—who define the uniqueness of Bowling Green.

I was a baby when my mother divorced my father. She and I returned to Bowling Green to live with my grandparents. I remember nothing about the divorce, but I do remember the love and care given me as a child in this small Kentucky town. My Granddaddy Sullivan, or Dynamite Dan to his friends, was my hero. He drove one of the big K4B Pacific steam locomotives on the L&N Railroad, and I thought Granddaddy walked on water. One of my favorite childhood memories is Grandmother taking me to the depot to see Granddaddy's train come in. I remember being scared of the smoke, steam and loud noise of the locomotive yet strangely drawn to it.

My trips on the Pullman car, especially the ones at night, were quite the adventure for a little boy. I recall looking out the window draped with a sleeping curtain to block the glare and letting my imagination run wild as the train raced across the countryside. "It feels as if we're flying, Grandmother," I said as the train sped over an elevated trestle or bridge. In my young and impressionable mind and heart, the sensation of flying had taken root.

Other vivid memories of growing up in Bowling Green center on the World War II era.

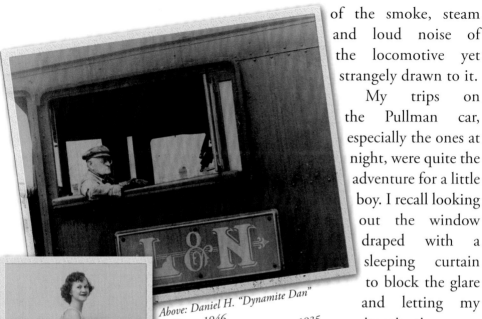

Above: Daniel H. "Dynamite Dan" Sullivan, 1946.

Left: Martha Sullivan Cherry, 1935.

Uniforms were everywhere. I noticed the soldiers, particularly the Army Air Forces pilots with their flashy silver wings, getting on and off the trains, shopping in the stores, and strolling through the town. Just like my grandfather Sullivan, they too became my role models and my aspiration.

By the time I was 10, Mother married her high school sweetheart. Henry Hardin Cherry, Jr. became my dad, and a great dad he was. As evidence of the love we shared, he adopted me and gave me the Cherry name—a blessing I will never forget. An aeronautical engineer, Dad moved us around a lot while he chased defense contracts. Henry Hardin Cherry, Jr. was not an aviator, but he worked on some amazing airplanes such as the F7U Cutlass, the B49 Flying Wing, the C-130 and the C-5A. We traveled from California to Texas and back again—finally residing in Powder Springs, Georgia. It was a great life, but Bowling Green continued to feel like home for our nomadic family.

Dan Cherry as Aviation Cadet Colonel, 1960.

Wherever we lived I remember airplanes constantly flying over our house. I imagined what fun it would be to fly the P-51 and the early jets like the F-80, the F-84 or the F-86. Through high school, the years I attended Western Kentucky University, and my early Air Force days as an Aviation Cadet, my love of airplanes grew. Finally, at age 20, a dream hatched by a little boy years earlier aboard the Pan American passenger train became a reality.

My 29 years in the Air Force were magical. I worked with wonderful people and flew fantastic airplanes such as the F-105, the F-4 and the F-16. I also had the great honor to command the Air Force Thunderbirds, the 8th Tactical Fighter Wing and the Air Force Recruiting Service. I will always be grateful to the Air Force for the opportunities it gave me and the lessons it taught me, but when retirement came in 1989, it was only natural for me to use Bowling Green as a springboard to a second career.

At my mother's insistence, my wife Syl and I temporarily moved in with her. We never expected to live permanently in Bowling Green, but the longer we stayed, the harder it became to leave. Doors opened to good job opportunities and

Dan, Syl, Jill and Kim Cherry, 1978.

AVIATION HERITAGE PARK

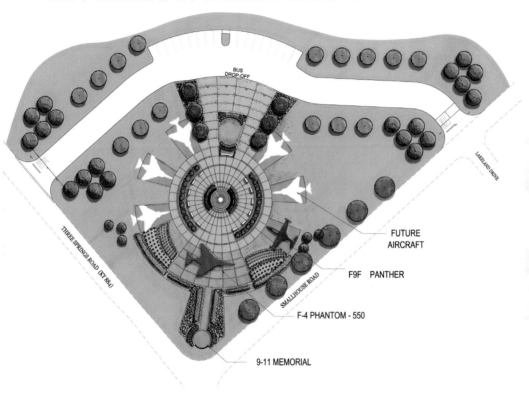

BUS DROP-OFF

THREE SPRINGS ROAD (KY 884)

SMALLHOUSE ROAD

LAKELAND DRIVE

FUTURE AIRCRAFT

F9F PANTHER

F-4 PHANTOM - 550

9-11 MEMORIAL

Architectural design by Arrasmith, Judd, Rapp, Chovan Inc.

Landscape design by Brian Shirley.

in almost no time we were once again surrounded by friendly people with the strong traditions I remembered from early childhood. Traditions of caring for each other, supporting the local businesses, and more importantly, giving back to the community.

It was in the spirit of "giving back" that the idea of Aviation Heritage Park was conceived. The roots of such an idea had already been deeply planted in the untold stories of Kentucky's aviation heroes. But the idea blossomed when we discovered and restored my airplane from the Vietnam War, the F-4D #66-7550, Phantom 550—the very airplane I was piloting in 1972 when I shot down a North Vietnamese MiG-21. Perhaps it was at that moment of discovery when a few good friends and I began to dream. And what we dreamed was big!

We dreamed about a facility, a park, designed to display aviation artifacts that would represent the real stories of real

Photograph of Aviation Heritage Park by Bob Pitchford, June 2009.

people. We imagined the unlimited uses such a facility would offer to our community. We considered how teachers could use the displays as educational tools of information to teach history, math and science; how such a community project could motivate and inspire the youth to reach for their dreams, to work hard, and to believe anything is possible for those who apply themselves.

It was the same message of motivation, *to believe anything is possible*, that inspired me to take a long awaited journey on behalf of Aviation Heritage Park—a journey that would take me half way around the world to Ho Chi Minh City (Saigon), Vietnam, in search of the vanquished MiG-21 pilot.

The dream of Aviation Heritage Park touched the hearts of so many in and around our community, and in their "giving-back" tradition, countless local citizens donated time and resources to make the project happen. The truth is evident; the Bowling Green community grabbed on to the ideas of a few and made those ideas a reality for all.

Johnny Magda's F9F-2 Panther. Illustration by Jack Morris, JDMC Aviation Graphics.

Western Kentucky University (WKU '40) graduate Johnny Magda boarding Blue Angel 1, January 1950.

The dedication ceremony is just around the corner, but don't wait to visit Aviation Heritage Park located at the corner of Three Springs and Smallhouse Roads. A beautiful place and a point of pride for all Kentuckians, it will tell the incredible stories of Victor Strahm, Johnny Magda, Russ Dougherty, Ken Fleenor, Terry Wilcutt and many more. We are certain you will feel the same sense of pride we do as you pause to honor the remarkable aviators from our past and use their stories to mold good citizens for our future.

www.aviationheritagepark.com

DISCOVERY

My Bowling Green Walking Group buddies are special people. For 20 years we have been getting up at the crack of dawn, gathering in a local neighborhood and walking at a very fast pace for three miles. We end up at McDonald's to have coffee and solve all the world's problems.

Over the years there have been several occasions when we planned trips. I have a vivid memory of a most fortuitous outing we planned in June 2004. We decided to take a weekend trip to Dayton, Ohio, to see the National Museum of the United States Air Force. We would rent a van, drive to Dayton, visit the museum and on the way home, stop in Cincinnati to see a baseball game. Nine of our members signed up. Early one Thursday morning, we headed for Dayton.

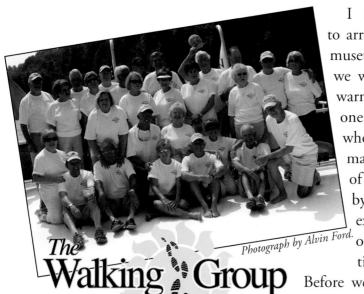

Photograph by Alvin Ford.

The
Walking Group

AN EARLY MORNING TRADITION   SINCE 1984

I had called ahead to arrange a tour of the museum. As soon as we walked in we were warmly greeted by one of the docents who guided us on a marvelous tour. All of us were captivated by the aircraft exhibits as well as other artifacts so time passed quickly. Before we left, several staff members chatted with us about the tour and our favorite exhibits. One staff member said, "You know, there's an airplane nearby that holds historical significance to Kentucky. It might become available."

Of course, our group was full of questions, but it was the answers we got from the staff that astounded us. The airplane in question fit the description of the F-4 Phantom I flew in Vietnam the day I scored an aerial victory over a MiG-21. The plane was on display at a Veterans of Foreign Wars (VFW) Club in Enon, Ohio, and apparently the club was having difficulty taking care of it. No promises were made, but since we were from Kentucky and I was in the group, the staff wanted us to know the circumstances in case an opportunity for acquisition might develop.

We left the museum and adjourned to the Officers' Club. The Phantom at Enon was all we talked about.

"Dan, you mean to tell us that this could be the actual airplane you flew and not just one like it?"

"If that tail number is 66-7550, it's the same one," I answered.

That night we agreed to locate the airplane and see it before we went home.

Checking the map, we determined that Enon was about 20 miles from Dayton, so at morning light we headed for Enon. One of the locals at a

Phantom 550 Enon, Ohio, June 2004.

Minit Mart provided specific directions. I sensed the anticipation in all of us as we passed small residential areas, farmland and pastoral fields. Suddenly our van rounded a sharp curve and we saw her. Painted gray. Grass growing up around her tires. We slowed our van to a crawl to get a better look, and there it was—the victory star—clearly visible near the engine intake. I felt as if I had unexpectedly found a long, lost friend.

The June morning was cooler than expected as I climbed out of the van and approached her. She seemed huge, much bigger than I remembered. I looked squarely at her tail number. "It's her all right," I called out. "There's the tail number I remember, 66-7550. She sure could use some major TLC." Birds had roosted in every nook and cranny and their droppings were everywhere. The tires were flat. Rust had eaten completely through

the fins on the inert 500-pound bombs mounted on her inboard pylons. It was sad to see her in such shameful condition, but I was thrilled to know she had not suffered major damage. The others bounded out of the van shouting questions as they joined me next to the airplane.

"Dan, what did that thing do?

"Where did you carry your missiles?

"What is that big round thing hanging under the belly? Boy, it's a lot bigger than I thought it would be."

I happily answered their questions. As we walked around her, I had a feeling of déjà vu—like I was her pilot again making a preflight inspection. When we stopped below the engine intake, our focus shifted to the red victory star on the splitter vane near the engine intake.

"Dan, you've got to tell us the story of that dogfight."

"What happened? Did you shoot the MiG down with a missile? What kind?"

"Do you remember that day? Dan, were you scared?"

My hand rested on the red star and I shivered in the cold morning air. Eight of my best friends were eagerly waiting to hear what I had to say.

"Remember," I muttered. "Yeah, I remember." I choked back the emotion.

Memories came flooding back to me—memories of a life-changing experience. In my mind it was April 16, 1972 all over again. For the first time I told my friends the story.

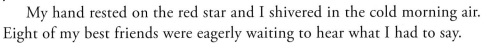

17°N

April 16, 1972.

The phone began to ring in my trailer at two o'clock that morning.

"Major Cherry, this is the command post. You need to report to the main briefing room at 0430."

"What's going on?" I asked, half asleep. "I'm on the Laredo schedule later in the day."

"You'll find out when you get here; just don't be late."

"Yes sir." I hung up the phone and reset my alarm in hopes of getting some more sleep. No chance. I could feel the excitement building. To change the entire flying schedule and to be called in the middle of the night meant it had to be something very unusual.

0430. I walked into a briefing room full of F-4 aircrews from all of the squadrons at Udorn. The map up on the briefing board clearly showed planned routes all the way to Hanoi. This was the biggest strike into the heart of North Vietnam since the bombing halt of 1968. Like everyone else, I felt excited but a bit apprehensive too. Rarely had any of us in recent years encountered the threats of MiGs, heavy antiaircraft fire or surface-to-air missiles. But this mission was going to be much more dangerous than we had become accustomed to.

I searched the briefing board for my name. There it was. The 13th Tactical Fighter Squadron Panther Pack, call sign Basco. I was flying Basco 3 with Jeff Feinstein in my back seat. My good friend Fred "Fredo" Olmsted was our flight leader with Stu Maas in his back seat. Basco 2 was Steve Cuthbert and Danny Souell. Basco 4 on my wing was Greg Crane and Gerry Lachman. I smiled. We had flown together before so I felt good about our chances for a successful mission.

Our mission was to escort another flight of bomb-laden F-4s from Korat Air Base as they proceeded to their target in the Hanoi area, but apparently Basco was a last minute add-on. The hard reality was we had no tanker support scheduled and less than a full load of missiles. Such circumstances were highly unusual for a mission into the heart of North Vietnam. As a result of the tanker shortage, our aircraft were configured with three external fuel tanks to give us the range and endurance needed to get to the target and back safely.

My eyes followed Fredo, watching for any signs of anxiety as he led the briefing. Fred Olmsted had already been credited with one MiG-21 kill, but this morning his emphasis was on mutual support and the admonition that no MiG kill in the world was worth losing a wingman. He explained his aircraft was equipped with a top-secret device that enabled his Weapons System Officer (WSO), Stu Maas, to interrogate the MiG's onboard radar transponder and to positively identify the MiG as hostile as soon as he had radar contact. Fredo emphasized that the Air Force had such confidence in this new technology that the rules of engagement had been changed to authorize us to shoot beyond visual range. I knew this technology gave us a huge advantage, but there would be more than 50 friendly airplanes in the same general area of our assignment. The last thing I wanted to do was shoot down one of my buddies.

We all discussed the new high-tech advantage at length and decided

13th Tactical Fighter Squadron, Udorn Royal Thai Air Base, 1972.

because the equipment was new, and none of us had actually used it in a combat situation, we wouldn't trust it enough to fire without a positive visual ID on the bogey. We agreed to stick together as a four-ship, but we would break up into elements and fight in two-ship formations if necessary. In the briefing we talked at length about fuel conservation and the fact that we were going to be a long way from home without any scheduled tanker support. Fredo emphasized we must watch our fuel closely and jettison our external fuel tanks at exactly the right time. "Our Bingo is 8,000 pounds," he said, "and, as soon as the first centerline goes dry, we're going to jettison them and we'll all do it together." There were very strict airspeed and G limitations for jettisoning that tank. It had to be done at slow speed before crossing the border into a high-threat area.

Briefing over, it was off to the personal equipment shop to pick up harness, g-suit, helmet, survival vest and side arm. I jumped in the shuttle van alongside the others and headed to my aircraft. That's when I first saw her—Phantom 550. There was nothing unusual about her appearance. Just one of our typical F-4Ds except for the PN on the tail. Seeing those letters, I knew she came from another squadron. She looked good in the early morning light. Jeff Feinstein and I checked her over closely. We noted five missiles loaded; three AIM-7 Sparrows and two AIM-9 Sidewinders. The other missile stations were taken up by Electronic Counter Measures (ECM) pods to help ward off the surface-to-air missiles we were sure to encounter.

With the preflight complete, Jeff and I climbed into the cockpit and strapped in. I turned the battery on, checked the intercom with him, started the engines and the big Phantom came to life. What a powerful sound she made! Two J-79's spooling up; generators switched on line, cockpit lights flashing and then the radio check. "Basco Flight, check in," was Fredo's call. "Two, three, four" came our team's response. We were ready to taxi. Chocks were pulled, power pushed up, and Phantom 550 rolled to the end of the runway for a last-minute check from our maintenance crew.

In my gut the butterflies and rapid breathing had begun. It was a familiar reaction, like the feeling the football player gets just before the first hit of the game. As a pilot, I knew it was normal to be apprehensive of dangers ahead but shook off the feeling and turned my eyes toward my crew chief. With an enthusiastic thumbs-up and a salute from him and a cleared-for-takeoff call from the tower; Basco flight pointed four noses down Udorn's runway 12 at 0730 on April 16, 1972. *What a great team,* I thought. *Confident and ready for whatever might come our way. Scared? Maybe a little scared, too.*

June 2004.

"Dan! Dan! Are you OK?" Someone was calling me.

"Where did you go? You suddenly got so quiet."

"You were telling us about Basco Flight and your mission near Hanoi, April 16, 1972."

"Oh yes, sorry," I said. "Guess I drifted off."

Standing in that grassy field near Enon, I was amazed how vivid the memories of that April day suddenly became. I once more allowed my hands to trace the curves and panels of the war machine that took such good care of me long ago.

"Dan? What about the dogfight? You were about to tell us about the dogfight."

Regaining my composure, I finally shared the dogfight story with my friends. Then, reluctantly, we got in the van and headed south for Cincinnati and Bowling Green.

Members of the Walking Group with the Phantom 550 in Enon, Ohio, June, 2004.

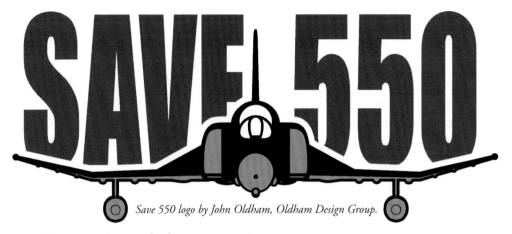

Save 550 logo by John Oldham, Oldham Design Group.

Once on the road, the conversation was nonstop.

"We've just got to get that airplane to Kentucky. It's a damn shame it hasn't been better taken care of."

"Wonder how much it would cost to move it, Dan?"

Needless to say, there was a lot of enthusiasm about what we might be able to do in the future, but I was quick to caution everyone. "Even if the long shot came through and the Air Force gave us permission to take possession of the aircraft," I said, "it would be a huge undertaking, costing thousands of dollars to move and restore it. How could we ever raise that kind of money, and where would we put it once we got it to Bowling Green?"

I wasn't trying to throw a wet blanket on the notion. I just wanted everyone to know the magnitude of the challenges: first, to move and restore it; then to take care of it in perpetuity. It would be a major long-term obligation.

But, the enthusiasm and conversation continued, and I suggested we meet with Ray Buckberry, a retired attorney and local historian. Ray had done some research on famous aviators from the Bowling Green area, and at a brainstorming session, Ray shared with us stories of some remarkable men. Men like Bert Hall, an ace in World War I and a member of the Lafayette Escadrille; Victor Strahm, also an ace in WW I and a general

Johnny Magda, Blue Angels Flight Leader, January, 1950.

in the early Army Air Service; Johnny Magda, an ace in WW II, world speed record holder in the early Navy jets, Flight Leader for the Navy Blue Angels and winner of the Navy Cross for heroic action during the Korean War; Ken Fleenor, a highly decorated Air Force general and F-4 pilot who was a prisoner of war for seven years; and Terry Wilcutt, a Marine Corps fighter pilot and space shuttle commander. "The sad part about these men and their stories," Ray said, "is very few people are aware of this wonderful heritage."

Amidst the discussions and the storytelling, everyone in our group kept

Famous Kentucky aviators illustration by Bob Pitchford.

asking the same questions. "What can we do to make more people aware of these stories, and how can we use the information in a constructive way?" The answer? Aviation Heritage Park. More discussion about a park led to more rhetorical questions. Why not establish an educational facility where aviation artifacts could be displayed to represent these stories—real stories, about real people, from our area? Why not acquire Phantom 550 as the first artifact and add more as resources permit? Would not an Aviation Heritage Park provide motivation and inspiration to our youth?

It became clear that the seed of an idea planted with the discovery of Phantom 550 had flowered into a much bigger vision. Beyond preserving and displaying my airplane, Aviation Heritage Park had become a broader educational tool designed to benefit the community for years to come.

The original group of planners bought in to the concept immediately. We established a nonprofit corporation and solicited the support of local

The dismantled Phantom 550 rolls into Bowling Green on a rainy December day, 2005.

government. Aviation Heritage Park was officially incorporated in January 2005. The city and county quickly passed resolutions of support and a formal application was submitted to the Air Force to take possession of Phantom 550.

In June 2005, the Air Force approved our application. The money was raised and the dismantled airplane arrived in Bowling Green on a rainy day in December, 2005. Restoration began immediately. After a good cleaning, sanding and paint job, Phantom 550 was returned to her original Vietnam era color scheme. The ugly duckling was transformed into the beautiful swan. Green and brown camouflage paint and perfect markings made her look exactly as she did in 1972. Restoring Phantom 550 was an important task, but equally important was the community's long-term commitment to protect her and always point to her as a source of pride for all to see.

While the restoration was in progress, our board members frequently discussed ways to raise money. Like other nonprofit organizations, we were always faced with the challenge of raising enough money to keep up with all the good ideas. On one occasion, someone asked jokingly, "Why don't we try to find out what happened to that MiG pilot you shot down, Dan? Can you imagine what would happen if the national media got involved? We would really be able to raise money from that story." All of us had a good laugh and continued to discuss other ways to get the funds we needed. But the idea of finding the MiG-21 pilot kept coming up again and again.

It never failed. Someone would mention the MiG I shot down and I would find myself remembering the last glimpse I had of the pilot. It was at the end of our dogfight. My missile had struck the MiG where the right wing joined the fuselage. The wounded aircraft was on fire and plummeting toward the ground. Suddenly, there he was. Suspended horizontally because of the speed, under his white parachute with one red panel—his black flight suit clearly visible. Who was this guy? I had never stopped wanting to know. What was his name? Did he have a family? Did he survive the bailout and return to fly again? For more than 30 years, I had filed away the memories of the MiG pilot, of Udorn, of Fredo, Jeff, Greg and Basco Flight. For more than 30 years, I had wrestled with the flashbacks of that day and my endless questions about the Vietnamese pilot. Would I ever know the answers?

Lou Drendel
1974

"The MiG That Didn't Get Away" by Lou Drendel.

BASCO FLIGHT

In 1971 the Air Force hung out a carrot to F-105 Thunderchief "Thud" drivers who had completed a 100 mission combat tour by offering a checkout in the F-4 to pilots volunteering for a second tour. I dearly loved the Thud, but the future in that airplane was bleak. Their numbers were dwindling fast due to combat losses, and there were nagging concerns: the unfinished business of an ongoing war and the reality that several good friends were being held as prisoners of war. It was a tough decision to leave the family and go into harm's way once again, but my intuition told me it was the right thing to do. Immediately, I departed for Homestead Air Force Base to check out in the F-4.

By June, I was on my way to Udorn Royal Thai Air Force Base, Thailand, and the 13th Tactical Fighter Squadron "Panther Pack." The missions consisted of two-ship bombing missions in Laos under the control

Dan and F-105 at Korat, Thailand, 1967.

of a Forward Air Controller (FAC), an occasional reconnaissance (recce) escort mission into the southern part of North Vietnam and the Laredo Fast FAC mission. I preferred to fly recce escorts because I felt we were doing something productive to protect the recce guys from MiGs. According to the rules of engagement (ROE), our pilots could actually drop bombs in North Vietnam if the recce airplane was fired upon.

This pattern of missions continued through 1971. Although most of our pilots yearned for more action, our schedule of missions gave us a chance to train and hone the skills of our younger, less experienced aircrews. After each mission we returned to Thai airspace and practiced tactical formation, breaks, rejoins and switchology until we were almost out of fuel. This schedule was grueling in the tropical climate of Southeast Asia, but it really paid off. It was gratifying to watch the young guys grow, gain confidence and come together as a team. When the war heated up, I knew the Panther Pack was ready.

As the calendar changed from 1971 to 1972, the combat missions assigned to our 432nd Tactical Reconnaissance Wing became progressively more challenging. The enemy reaction to our reconnaissance flights increased significantly. For the first time since 1968 we were assigned multiple flight bombing missions to specific targets in the lower part of North Vietnam. None of the assigned targets were in the northern, more heavily defended part of the country until April 15 when the Air Tasking Order (FRAG) for the next day came in. It called for us to launch 20 airplanes providing MiG Combat Air Patrol (MIGCAP) in the Hanoi area for multiple bombing flights from the other F-4 and F-105 bases.

Udorn had the primary responsibility to provide protection from enemy aircraft so the strike flights from other bases could fly deep into North Vietnam. Our flight, "Basco," led by Fred Olmsted and Stu Maas was assigned to provide MIGCAP support to a secondary flight of Phantoms from Korat Air Base. We were to rendezvous with the bomb-laden Korat F-4s over northern Laos and proceed to the target. Since ours was a secondary strike and the primary effort included a lot of airplanes, we had no tanker support. There just were not enough support aircraft to go around.

At 0730, Basco Flight taxied on to Udorn's runway 12, lit the afterburners and roared off into a hazy early-morning sky. Each airplane

"Spook," courtesy of Phantom II Society.

was configured with a 600-gallon centerline tank, two 370-gallon wing tanks, two Sidewinder heat-seeking missiles, three radar-guided Sparrow missiles and two ECM pods. With all that fuel and armament on board, each F-4 weighed over 50,000 pounds.

After takeoff and join-up, we proceeded north into Laos, reached the rendezvous point over the Laotian village of Ban Ban and began to orbit while we waited for the strike flight to arrive. The minutes dragged by with no sign of the Korat flight so we began to calculate our options if our primary mission canceled. If we waited much longer our low fuel state would preclude any combat action. Finally, with our fuel at a critical point, Fredo decided to proceed with our secondary mission which was to patrol for MiG targets of opportunity in an area about 30 miles southwest of Hanoi.

Our centerline external fuel tanks began to run dry and remembering the very stringent G and airspeed limitations for jettisoning that tank Fredo pulled his nose up and the rest of us followed. We climbed, slowed down, and punched off all four tanks in unison. Then the noses came down, the power came up and we turned to put Hanoi on the nose as we picked up speed for our dash into North Vietnam.

As soon as we crossed the border into North Vietnam we picked up surface-to-air missile (SAM) and antiaircraft radar strobes on our radar warning gear. The enemy was locking on to us as we searched visually for SAM launches and on the radar for MiGs. The Navy had the primary responsibility for the coastal areas; we didn't want to infringe upon their territory, so we turned due south midway into North Vietnam. We flew in a tactical spread formation to an area we called the Fish's Mouth, an area where Route 7 extends into Laos, all the while searching for any bad guys. When we reached Route 7 we turned 180 degrees and headed north toward Yen Bai airfield west of Hanoi.

That's when it started. Stu Maas in the back seat of Olmsted's airplane picked up two bandits on his radar at 20 miles. "Basco has two bandits on the nose for twenty," was Stu's radio call. We turned slightly putting the bandits on the nose. Then Fredo called, "Let's get rid of 'em, Basco." Eight external wing tanks immediately separated from our Phantoms. We increased power to gain more speed. Stu maintained his radar contact and called out the range as we closed to fifteen…ten…five and then we picked them up visually.

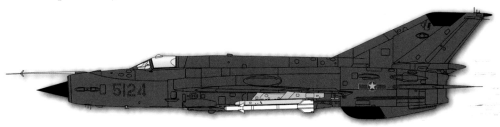

MiG-21 illustration by Jack Morris, JDMC Aviation Graphics.

Phantom 550 photo illustration by John Fleck.

"There's a MiG-21 there Dan!" Fredo exclaimed. Sure enough, two silver MiG-21's passed over us about 5,000 feet higher than we were and on a reciprocal heading. Olmsted called for a hard right turn and we cranked it around, trying to keep the two MiGs in sight. I was on the outside of the turn leading the second element, so I fell behind on the turn away from me. Halfway through the turn, my wingman Greg "Baby Beef" Crane called out a third MiG at twelve o'clock level to me and climbing into position behind Olmsted's element. It was a camouflaged MiG-21 closing fast. Apparently the North Vietnamese had set a trap using the two silver MiGs for bait. The camouflaged MiG stayed low and as we started our turn he climbed and accelerated hoping to roll in behind us as we chased the silver bandits.

I rolled out of the turn and headed directly for the camouflaged MiG giving my WSO Jeff Feinstein a running commentary on the MiG's position so he could try to acquire him on radar. The MiG pilot saw us and turned hard left directly into a cloud. The tops of the clouds reached 15,000 feet, and we were skimming them at 450 knots when the MiG disappeared. I thought to myself, *I'll never see him again,* but I figured I might as well go in the clouds after him. We might get lucky and acquire him on radar or spot him on the other side of the cloud bank.

After what seemed like hours in the clouds searching for the bandit on radar, I got nervous and pulled up. The threat of SAMs around Hanoi was significant and our primary defense was early visual acquisition in order to take evasive action

Illustration by Phantom II Society.

and outmaneuver the missile. The more time we spent in the clouds, the less chance we would have to see a missile coming at us. Finally, we popped out on top of the cloud bank and searched the horizon in all directions. We didn't see a thing. I thought, *we lost him for sure.*

In the meantime, Olmsted and his wingman were still in hot pursuit of the other two MiGs. I made a hard right turn in the direction I had last seen Olmsted heading. As we rolled out of the turn, my hawk-eyed

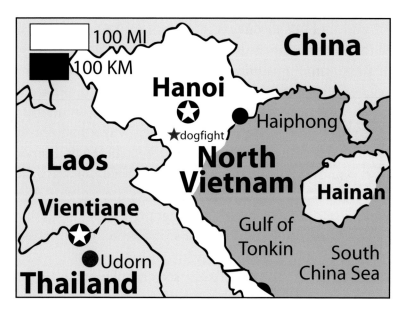

wingman Baby Beef Crane spotted our MiG again. "Two o'clock high. He's right above you, Dan," Greg called. And there he was, at two o'clock and 5,000 feet above us in a climbing right turn. I picked him up visually, went to max afterburner and pulled up to get into firing position. As the nose of Phantom 550 tracked toward the target, I had a beautiful set-up for a heat-seeking Sidewinder shot. The sun was behind us and there was nothing except the MiG and blue sky in front of us. I pulled the nose out in front of him, selected HEAT to arm the missiles and pulled the trigger. Nothing happened. I squeezed again...still nothing. Rechecked the armament switches...all OK...squeezed again...nothing...squeezed again…still nothing. Despair. I was in perfect position—a situation that I had waited for all my life—and I had a bad fire control system.

I maintained good position behind the MiG as he climbed above 25,000 feet over the top and started down in a diving spiral trying his best to get away. Baby Beef was out about a 1,000 feet, in perfect fighting wing formation. I knew he must be wondering why I had not taken the shot when I had the chance. At that point, my confidence in my aircraft's fire control system was shattered. When Greg called out, "I'm taking the lead, passing on the left," I acknowledged, "Roger Beef, you've got it." I rolled around Greg into fighting wing formation as he lined up the MiG in his sights and started firing his missiles. His first Sparrow malfunctioned and fell away like a bomb. His next one went into a corkscrew spiral and missed the MiG by a mile. Greg and Gerry Lachman couldn't get a radar lock-on and consequently were firing in the bore sight mode with the radar slaved to the axis of the aircraft. Beef smoothly tracked the MiG in his

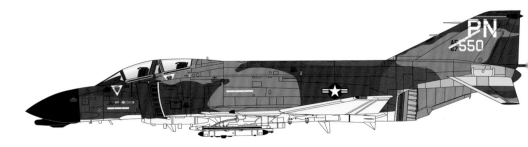

Phantom 550 illustration by Jack Morris, JDMC Aviation Graphics.

gun sight—keeping him highlighted in the radar beam—and fired his last missile. It tracked perfectly, heading straight for the MiG. Exactly at the critical point in time prior to missile impact, the MiG pilot performed a break maneuver by turning hard into the attack. The Sparrow cruised right by his tailpipe without detonating.

Pushing my fears aside, I calculated my enemy's next move. I knew his hard break maneuver dissipated all his energy and we would maintain the advantage. Just one obstacle stood in the way of a kill: lack of fire power. All we had left were my three Sparrows and no assurances they would fire. I made up my mind to stay at his six o'clock and vowed he would not get away from us. Even if my Sparrows didn't fire, I would chase him until I hit "bingo" (minimum fuel state) and then run for home. I also remember thinking if my missiles failed to fire, I might try to ram him. In hindsight, it would have been a foolish move, but it accurately reflects my aggressive, must-win attitude at the time.

I radioed Greg that I was taking back the lead. No answer. "Basco 4, break left!" Still, no answer. We were both in max afterburner (AB) so I couldn't easily overtake him, and he was too far out in front for me to risk the shot. I certainly didn't want to hit him by mistake. I continued trying to pass and take the lead, calling him again to break out of the way so I could shoot.

Distinguished Flying Cross Medal.

"Break left, Beef, I've got him wired!" I yelled.

I called Jeff in the back seat. "I've got the pipper right on him, Jeff. Lock him up!" Immediately Jeff performed his radar magic and the analog bar popped out on the edge of the gun sight indicating a good radar lock-on.

It seemed to take forever for me to pull up line abreast with Greg. When I did regain lead of our two-ship formation, Greg called, "Go get him Dan!" I clamped down on the trigger. *Whoosh!* To my amazement, the big AIM-7 Sparrow smoked out in front of us. We were in a right descending turn, accelerating through 500 knots and closing on the MiG as the missile fired. It did a big barrel roll and appeared to travel too far out in front of him. I realized it was just pulling lead. The missile rapidly closed the 4,000 foot distance and struck the MiG in the area where the right wing joins the fuselage, exploding in a huge fireball. "Got him! I got him!" I shouted.

The explosion blew the right wing completely off the MiG and it immediately went into a hard spin trailing fire and smoke. After one turn of the spin, the MiG pilot ejected and his parachute opened directly in front of me. I quickly turned away to avoid flying through the chute. I also wanted to be sure that Jeff could see the MiG pilot and his airplane going down in flames. There were too many pilots who failed to get credit for their kills because no one else saw them. We had a lot of good witnesses that day.

The whole experience had a dreamlike quality about it. *This is like in the movies*, I thought. There we were, smoking by this guy just as his parachute opened. We must have been almost supersonic with the afterburners cooking, and I knew we were no more than a hundred feet away from him when we passed. Even then I got a good look at him and distinctly remember his black flying suit and his white parachute with one red panel.

We could still hear Olmsted's element. He must have been close to us but cloud cover kept us from seeing him. Within a minute of my victory,

Jeff Feinstein, Dan, Fred Olmsted and Stu Maas after the kills, April 16, 1972.

he locked onto one of the silver MiGs. The MiG leader had rolled inverted, headed for the ground and run away, but the wingman seemed disoriented. Fredo knocked off the outer half of the MiG's right wing with his first missile, and the MiG went into a hard descending left turn. Fredo pulled up to gain separation, descended and fired a second AIM-7. His second missile hit the MiG dead center. It exploded in a huge fireball, leaving nothing but fluttering debris. I'll never forget Fredo's radio call to our controlling agency. "Disco, this is Basco. Scratch another MiG-21."

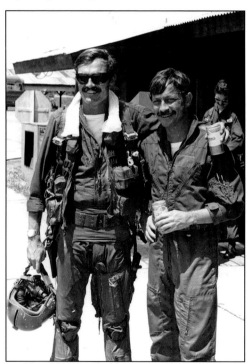

Fred "Fredo" Olmsted and Dan, April 16, 1972.

By this time we were low on fuel and I had one thought. *Let's get the hell out of here before more MiGs show up!* We did not have enough fuel or missiles to fight again that day. We dove for the deck, leveling off just above the treetops and headed for Udorn. Checking our fuel state, we considered trying to find a tanker, but there were too many guys egressing North Vietnam who really needed the gas.

We did our best to economize on our fuel consumption and pressed for home. Remarkably, we all landed safely with less than 15 minutes of fuel remaining.

I was proud to be part of Basco flight that day. Our leader had shown great courage, the flight members had been thoroughly trained and briefed, and we did exactly what we said we would do. We had flown the entire mission with only our original fuel load, shot down two MiGs after a five-minute dogfight—without help from radar controllers—and arrived home safe and sound.

That memorable day began my love affair with F-4D #66-7550, Phantom 550. Although I never flew her again, one never really forgets true love. Our paths would cross again three decades later in a grassy field near Dayton, Ohio.

Phantom 550 at Yokota Air Base Japan, 1972.

FULL CIRCLE

I n December 2005, 33 years after Basco Flight breached the skies over Hanoi, Phantom 550 rolled into Bowling Green, Kentucky, on two flatbed trailers. What a thrill to see her finally arrive at her new home. The trip from Enon, Ohio, went smoothly and our crew from Worldwide Aircraft Recovery expertly maneuvered her to a parking spot.

Getting her loaded on the trailers was quite a chore. The entire one-piece wing along with the horizontal stabilator and the external wing tanks had to be removed from the fuselage. A daunting task but our crew had done it before and in spite of the cold temperatures and icy conditions they had her disassembled, loaded and rolling down I-65 in short order. Reassembly was another challenge but that too was handled quickly and by December 7 she was all back together again at the Bowling Green-Warren County Regional Airport.

Since 1990, the airplane had been on display outside in Enon, Ohio. Encrusted bird droppings and nesting materials were everywhere. Power washing was the first step. Two days of hosing off the grime and removing the trash from the cockpits made her look clean as a whistle. The next step was to sand the entire airplane to remove any chipped paint or corrosion to get her ready for the primer coat. After sanding and another power washing, we were ready to paint.

Sherwin-Williams was kind enough to supply us with their best epoxy paint. In May, once the weather warmed, Davy Bowles of On-Site Painting used electrostatic paint guns to coat the airplane. The first coat, a primer, covered the entire aircraft, followed by the green and brown camouflage paint. To our good fortune, we had acquired an excellent color photograph of 550 taken in 1972. The photo provided us an accurate guide for duplicating exactly the historical colors and markings. In addition to the photograph, we also had JDMC Aviation Graphics' wonderful illustrations for the painters to use as they applied one color after the other. I even had Jack Morris' profile illustration enlarged and mounted on foam board so Davy would know exactly where the green stopped and the

Restored Phantom 550 by Biff Kummer.

brown began. Then came the numbers and markings recreated flawlessly in vinyl by Mike Fevold of Signature Signs. It was important to everyone involved that Phantom 550 look just right.

We unveiled the airplane in June 2006, at our annual Hangar Party. There were

Phantom 550 unveiling, June 2006.

gasps of approval as the fire department lifted off the huge parachute exposing the beautifully painted Phantom. Although she couldn't fly, she certainly looked like she could. On that day, Phantom 550 had her "coming out" party—a chance for her to shine. It was evident the citizens of Bowling Green warmly received her not only for her past meritorious service to her country but for her future service as an educational tool and inspiration to young people in years to come.

After the unveiling, Phantom 550 was put on temporary display at the Bowling Green airport as site selection and the conceptual design of the park got underway. Architectural expertise was donated by John Chovan of Arrasmith, Rapp, Judd, and Chovan, and his beautiful design fit perfectly on the four-acre site donated by the Warren County Fiscal Court. Excitement continued to build as the design was refined and more people became aware of the potential of the project and the importance of the park to the community's future.

A groundbreaking ceremony was held on April 16, 2007, the anniversary of Phantom 550's dogfight and aerial victory. Numerous dignitaries, business and political leaders were in attendance as ceremonial shovels turned the dirt and visions of the future beauty of this special place started to take shape.

Phantom 550 moving down Three Springs Road to Aviation Heritage Park, August 2007 photo by Bob Pitchford.

Moving Phantom 550 to her exhibit spot at the park required detailed planning. Public highways had to be traversed to get the airplane the three miles from the airport to the park. At 11:30 PM on a Sunday night, Phantom 550, wings folded, was hitched to a large tractor and rolled off airport property. A convoy of law enforcement and utility vehicles escorted her. It took two and a half hours to successfully dodge the mailboxes and avoid the overhead power lines. We all breathed a collective sigh of relief once she left the highway and settled in her permanent parking spot.

Lieutenant Nguyen Hong My and his MiG-21.

Although building the park and restoring the aircraft required much of our time, there were multiple brainstorming sessions as my friends and I discussed ideas on how to promote the park and how to pay for construction and restoration of additional artifacts. Time and again one idea kept surfacing—what if we could find the MiG pilot I shot down and invite him to the United States? It was such a long shot, the idea seemed laughable, but truth be told, I had always been curious about the fate of the MiG pilot. So the decision was made to launch a serious investigation to find out anything we could about him.

Inquiries through several business connections brought no results until a friend, Ed Faye, whose Vietnamese friends still had family in Vietnam, alerted me to a popular television show there called "The Separation Never Seems to Have Existed." The premise behind the show was to reunite people who had been separated for various reasons. After the show's producer heard of my quest to find out more about the MiG pilot, she sent an e-mail asking me to write a letter stating my intentions and describing the circumstance surrounding the dogfight. I quickly complied. Within two weeks I received another e-mail from her stating they had found the "brave MiG pilot" and inviting me to Vietnam to appear with him on television.

Producer Thu Uyen Nguyen-Pham.

I vacillated between excitement and skepticism as I acknowledged the possibility of flying to Vietnam to meet the MiG pilot on the television show. It was vitally important for me to be sure the TV show was legitimate with no hidden agenda or ulterior motives. I was also concerned about how former POWs might feel about my participation. Inquiries through the U. S. Embassy and some of my POW friends gave me the confidence I needed to accept the invitation. I boarded United Air Lines in Nashville, Tennessee—destination Ho Chi Minh City (Saigon).

April 5, 2008, Mr. Hong My and I met each other for the first time on live national television. My heart was pounding as he walked onto the set. We immediately locked eyes as he approached me with a very pleasant look on his face. He greeted me with a firm handshake and words of welcome; he expressed his pleasure that I was in good health and his hope that we would become friends. I responded with similar comments and we sat down around a table with the host-producer Thu Uyen.

Dan and Hong My, first handshake, April 2008.

News conference after the TV show, April 2008.

The television interview began with prerecorded information about our families. Tears came to my eyes as I watched pictures of my children and grandchildren flash on the monitor. I noticed that Hong My reacted in the same manner when pictures of his family appeared. There we sat, two tough old fighter pilots, crying on national television. It was clear; the chemistry between us was good right from the start.

After the show ended, we adjourned to the roof top of the Majestic Hotel in Saigon where we dined, drank wine and, with the help of an interpreter, got to know one another. We talked about all the usual things pilots talk about. I learned Hong My had spent four years in the Soviet Union in the early 1960s going through pilot training and checking out in the MiG-21. His pilot wings had been presented to him personally by

Ho Chi Minh, and he had been credited with one American victory in January, 1972. He also shared with me that he had been badly injured in the ejection from his MiG during the dogfight. Both his arms had been broken, his back severely injured, but he recovered enough to fly again for another two years.

As I look back on the trip to Vietnam and time spent getting to know Hong My, I am reminded of the amazing events that occurred, one after another. One came when Hong My invited me to come to his home in Hanoi. I had already

Dan, Hong My and Larry Bailey on Vietnam Airlines from Saigon to Hanoi.

planned to travel to Hanoi the next day, so after I disclosed my travel plans, Hong My changed his own airline reservation in order to fly with me from Saigon to Hanoi. Admittedly, it felt strange flying on Vietnam Airlines over the same countryside where I had flown countless combat missions. Only this time, my former adversary was by my side in the airplane.

Upon our arrival in Hanoi, Hong My asked me if I would mind

Nguyen Hong My by Allen Polt.

walking to his house; it was very close to my hotel. Through the streets of Hanoi we walked, dodging motor scooters and passing the beautiful old French Opera House. Along the way people recognized Hong My and stopped to shake his hand. I think the television show, aired the night before, had

Hong Duc and Dan, April 2008.

made him an instant celebrity, but it was obvious to me that everyone in his neighborhood held him in very high esteem.

At his home I was introduced to his son Quan; Giang, Quan's wife; and Hong My's 1-year-old grandson, Duc, who was celebrating his first birthday that day. I also met Hong My's daughter Giang and her husband Phuong. Hong My had been holding little Duc in his arms during the introductions, but, as I moved closer, the little boy reached out to me. Without a moment's hesitation, Hong My handed Duc to me. The significance of that act filled me with warmth as I recognized the trust and confidence that had so quickly developed between the two of us.

After we enjoyed a delicious Vietnamese dinner, Hong My offered me a ride to my hotel on the back of his motor scooter—primary transportation for most everyone in Vietnam. What a sight we must have been at 11:00 PM—the MiG pilot and the F-4 pilot zipping through the streets of Hanoi, laughing, dodging traffic, and having a grand old time of it!

Dan and Hong My, Hanoi, Vietnam, April 2008.

Ho Chi Minh Mausoleum, Hanoi, Vietnam, April 2008.

I was still trying to digest what had happened the last few days when I agreed to join Hong My for a tour around Hanoi. He had offered to serve as my guide, and the experience of seeing his city through his eyes was incredible. I believe we visited every museum, war memorial and tourist spot the city had to offer. But it was our visit to the infamous "Hanoi Hilton" that proved to be the most interesting and the most emotional experience for me. Hoa Lo Prison, now a museum and tourist attraction, was built by the French at the turn of the century when Vietnam was a French colony. Most of the exhibits depicted how the French imprisoned Vietnamese citizens who fought for independence, but there were a few small exhibits showing American POWs during their incarceration.

Hoa Lo Prison

It was while we toured Hoa Lo Prison that I noticed a distinct change in the demeanor of Hong My. For most of our day he had been a happy and gregarious tour guide directing me in and out of the tourist attractions of Hanoi. Once inside the prison, he became quiet and somber. I think he understood how hard it was for me to walk through some of the same rooms where many of my good friends had suffered. As I paused to look at photographs of American POWs in one of the exhibits, Hong My quietly came up to me and whispered in my ear, "Did you have friends in here?" I answered, "Yes, I did." I pointed to a picture of John Flynn. "He is my friend." Hong My quietly lowered his eyes and shook his head.

As I emerged from the "Hanoi Hilton," I was overcome by a feeling of sorrow at the thought of what our American prisoners had endured at the hands of our enemy. Just standing in front of that horrible place brought tears to my eyes. Sensing my emotion, Hong My walked over to me, put his arm consolingly around my shoulder and patted me on the back.

In April, 1972, Hong My and I had met as enemies in the skies over North Vietnam. Thirty-six years later to the month, we had come full circle. That day, on the streets of Hanoi, my enemy had truly become my friend.

Dan and Hong My, Hanoi, Vietnam, April 2008.

EPILOGUE

As the two of us parted company on the streets of Hanoi, Hong My and I shook hands warmly, said our goodbyes and expressed our mutual hopes that we would see each other again soon. I thanked my new friend for his warm hospitality and extended an invitation for him to visit my home in the United States. He readily accepted and then asked me a personal favor. "When you get back to United States will you do research for me?" he said. "What kind of research?" I replied. "I would like to know more about the American pilot I shot down. If he survived, I would like to meet him and if he didn't survive I would like to express my sincere condolences to his family."

Hong My further explained that he had been credited with a victory over an American RF-4 on January 19, 1972. The dogfight occurred about 10:00 AM over Nghe An Province near Route 7 in an area known as the

Fish's Mouth. Hong My fired two missiles from his MiG-21 and watched as the RF-4 exploded into two pieces. He was extremely low on fuel and immediately turned away to return to his base. He did not see anyone bail out of the RF-4 and thought that in all likelihood the Americans had been killed. I could tell by his body language that Hong My was very sincere and I vowed to do all I could to find out more about the fate of the American aircrew.

I left Vietnam the next day amazed at what had happened to me over the past few days. My dream of reconciliation with my former enemy had come true and my hope that we would become friends and have a lot in common as professional military aviators was fulfilled.

Even though I was exhausted I could hardly sleep during the long flight home. So many remarkable events and amazing experiences were going through my mind that only the word providential seemed appropriate. This wonderful chain of events just could not have happened by accident.

Hong My at the Vietnamese Peoples Air Force Museum, Hanoi, Vietnam, April 2008.

Phantom 550 in flight over Oklahoma, 1985.

I thought about the career of Phantom 550, beginning with Air Force acceptance in 1967, surviving countless hours of combat duty in the early 1970s, and somehow finding her way to Wright-Patterson Air Force Base, Ohio, where she flew her last mission in 1989. And then there was the structural problem that precluded her movement to the Arizona boneyard and kept her in Ohio. The serendipitous trip I took to Dayton, finding her neglected in a grassy field, was the next event that seemed meant to be. The willingness of the Air Force to loan Phantom 550 to Warren County, Kentucky, for display, and the community support that materialized enabling her movement and restoration also seemed preordained.

The happenstance meeting with an old friend who was able to facilitate the full circle meeting with Hong My in Vietnam was the most incredible event of all. What are the odds that this unbelievable chain, started so long ago, would continue with such remarkable results? And now the possibility of a "Double Full Circle," where Hong My is able to meet his vanquished American aircrew? I couldn't wait to get home and start the research.

I also couldn't help but marvel at the wonderful treatment I received during my visit to Vietnam. The warmth of the Vietnamese people, the good chemistry between Hong My and me, and the general positive feeling I had about Vietnam's future made a big impression on me.

Once at home, after resting a few days, I got busy making inquiries about the circumstances surrounding Hong My's claimed victory. I called and e-mailed the Air Force Historic Research Agency at Maxwell Air Force Base and they were most helpful. I discovered that an RF-4, tail number 68-0573, was lost at approximately 9:55 AM on January 20 crashing in Laos near Route 7 not far from the Vietnam border. The pilot was Major Bob Mock and his navigator was Lt. John Stiles. Both men were rescued; the loss was attributed to ground fire. I examined the records of American losses several days either side of Hong My's claim and there was nothing that even came close in terms of aircraft type, time of day, and location. Even though the date was one day off, that could easily be attributed to a record keeping error.

My next step was to make contact with Bob Mock and John Stiles to confirm the circumstances and get their personal views about the possibility that a MiG, not ground fire, had shot them down. I remembered Bob and John from my days at Udorn in 1972. Our squadrons were right across the street from each other and we had flown together several times with me acting as fighter escort for their reconnaissance flights.

Sadly, my Google search revealed that Bob Mock had been killed in an automobile accident only two months earlier. However, I discovered John Stiles was alive and well and living in North Carolina. "John, this is Dan Cherry. Do you remember me?" I said when he answered the phone. "I sure do, Dan. You were in the 13th Squadron and escorted me on several missions." We exchanged pleasantries, got caught up on each other's lives since the war and then I asked the improbable question. "John, do you think it is possible that you and Bob were shot down by a MiG and not ground fire?" "It is certainly possible, Dan, but we were taking quite a bit of 37 mm antiaircraft fire at the time. I know that for sure." And that's where we left it. After more research and e-mail exchanges with Hong My and John, I am 98 percent sure that Hong My shot down John Stiles. We may never be absolutely certain but the most important thing to Hong My is that no one died and both crew members were rescued with only minor injuries.

Telling this story has not been easy for me. It seems there is too much ME in it; but it did happen this way and my hope is that telling it publicly will help others in some way. I hope that the fact that Nguyen Hong My and I were able to reconcile our wartime differences and become friends after a life-and-death dogfight might help other Vietnam veterans as they struggle for closure of their war experience. I am also hopeful that the lessons learned from our encounter might be an inspiration to our two countries to work hard for improved economic and cultural relations. The Vietnamese people should certainly be on our bestfriends list. There are also some important life lessons here for anyone, such as the futility of holding a grudge and the advisability of moving on and letting go of the past, no matter how unpleasant.

As this book goes to press, Hong My and his son Quan are scheduled to arrive in Bowling Green, Kentucky on April 16, 2009, the 37th anniversary of our dogfight and 35 years after the end of the Vietnam War. It is my hope that John Stiles will be here to meet him and complete this double full circle. I also look forward to the opportunity of introducing my family to Nguyen Hong My, at one time my enemy, now my friend.

April 14, 2009

The arrangements for Nguyen Hong My and his son Nguyen Hong Quan to visit the United States have gone very well. All the planning, worrying, and strategizing are over and their flight is scheduled to arrive at the airport in Nashville, Tennessee. Though the itinerary for the next two weeks is complicated, I am hopeful the end result will be a positive experience for everyone.

Nguyen Hong My, April, 2009.

While driving from Bowling Green to Nashville, I cannot help but recall events that have led to this historic day. My pastor, Dr. Paul Fryman, says the events are providential and I believe he is right. I remember my first meeting with Hong My—the dogfight over North Vietnam; the unorthodox radio calls between me and my wingman "Baby Beef" Crane; my Sparrow missile that blew Hong My's MiG-21 out from under him; Hong My's ejection from his fiery aircraft; his parachute floating down in front of my eyes. Admittedly, the last thing on my mind that fateful day was the future friendship he and I would share—that he would come to the United States, meet my family and have dinner with us in our home.

My mind races as I think about the circumstances leading me to the discovery and restoration of Phantom 550; the establishment of Aviation Heritage Park and my trip to Vietnam to meet the vanquished pilot, Nguyen Hong My, for the second time in our lives.

As I approach the entrance to the Nashville airport, my thoughts shift to the promises I made Hong My before leaving Vietnam one year ago. First, I promised I would do everything in my power to research and confirm the fate of the American aircrew Hong My was credited with shooting down in January, 1972. Second, I promised I would make arrangements for Hong My to visit the United States. Gratefully, I can say I honored both promises.

One of the highlights planned during Hong My's visit is the meeting between Hong My and John Stiles, the RF-4 aircrew member Hong My shot down. I owe so much to Anne O'Conner, archivist at the Air Force Historic Research Agency, for digging through the archives searching for the facts to identify John Stiles. Everything we discovered led to the same conclusion. Yet, resurrecting the past has not been a pleasant experience for John.

John Stiles, 1971.

"Dan, I stored those traumatic memories away long ago," exclaims John, "and now you come along and bring them all back up again."

John and I would have many conversations about how the Hong My story of reconciliation has been so well received and how important hearing the story is to other Vietnam veterans. John's response to all the new information concerning his downed flight near Nghe An Province is understandable.

"I feel certain that Hong My

shot us down," admits John, "but I really need to meet him before I know for sure."

I believe if we can pull off this reunion, it will be extremely important to both men!

The greeting party at the Nashville Airport consists of my wife Syl; John Fleck the photographer and good friend responsible for documenting this story; and Phuong Vu, Western Kentucky University graduate student acting as our interpreter. From a distance I can see Hong My and Quan making their way from the gate and looking "no worse for wear" after the long, grueling flight from Vietnam.

Dan and Hong My, Nashville Airport, April, 2009.

We approach each other with big smiles, shake hands warmly and hug. "Welcome to America," I say in both English and well-coached Vietnamese. The Nashville television stations are out in force, and after their interviews we begin our short drive to Bowling Green. The trip is great fun and with the help of Phuong Vu, we talk non-stop all the way.

"When am I going to meet the rest of your family?" Hong My asks.

"Tomorrow," I reply. "We will have dinner in my home tomorrow and you will get to meet them all."

Arriving at the Bowling Green hotel, I help Hong My and Quan unload their luggage, find their rooms and, before I leave them for the evening, I present small bags of welcome gifts. In the bag and on top of the other gifts, I have included a copy of the first edition of my book, *My Enemy…My Friend.*

"Hong My, this is for you; I hope you enjoy reading it." (Hong My reads English quite well.) "Rest now and I will pick you up first thing in the morning. Good night, my friend."

The next morning I join Hong My for breakfast in the hotel, and as we sit down at the table he says to me, "I don't like your book." I am crushed! Above all, I want Hong My's approval. My book has been a labor of love, something to be proud of, and I want him to like it in spite of the horrific outcome of our first meeting. Where did I go wrong? Did I say anything to offend him? Was something lost in the translation? I had received the first copies of the completed book from the printer a few weeks before Hong My's arrival. It was my intention to keep it a secret from him because I wanted to surprise him with a copy when he arrived.

Hong My with Dan's children and grandchildren, April, 2009.

At this point, it looks as if I am making a monumental mistake with the potential of getting his first visit to the United States off on the wrong foot.

So much has gone into the plans to bring Hong My to the United States. Regardless of his response to my book, I am determined to help him and Quan feel welcome and excited about the upcoming events. Earlier, the Aviation Heritage Park Board of Directors had endorsed the idea of raising the money necessary for Hong My's visit to coincide with the 37th anniversary of our dogfight, April 16, 2009, and the grand opening and dedication ceremony of Bowling Green's Aviation Heritage Park. Our itinerary, carefully drafted and approved by the board of directors, includes several days in Kentucky, a trip to Lakeland, Florida—the Sun 'n Fun Fly-In, and a trip to our nation's capital. I have kept John Stiles informed of the plans. John and I vow to do everything possible to arrange a meeting between him and Hong My during our time in Washington DC.

Two Weeks Later

Memories of the last two weeks crowd out the morning sounds of Washington D.C. waking up to a new day. I seem to move in slow motion as I help load the luggage into the waiting taxi. Hong My and Quan are scheduled to depart from Dulles International Airport for Vietnam. We have been together for two weeks, sometimes under stressful circumstances; yet, our friendship has endured and become even stronger. My memories of all the special people and historical events are reminders of how much has

Dan and Steve Hartman of CBS News, April, 2009.

happened in the days since Hong My and Quan arrived in the U.S.

The first week of their visit in Kentucky made me proud of my community, state and country. I know Hong My was impressed with his first taste of southern hospitality. He and Quan received warm, sincere welcomes while appearing for numerous local, regional and national media interviews including an interview with Steve Hartman of the *CBS Evening News*.

My wife Syl and I hosted a traditional southern family dinner in our home. Though our Vietnamese guests seemed to enjoy the food she prepared especially for them, Hong My much preferred to talk to my

Hong My and Quan in cockpit of Phantom 550, April 16, 2009.

children and grandchildren and present them with gifts. He has a special rapport with children of all ages, and they respond in love towards him, too.

Other Bowling Green events included the Aviation Heritage Park dedication ceremony where on April 16—for the first time in history—a vanquished fighter pilot returned to actually sit in the cockpit of the very airplane (Phantom 550) that shot him down.

The following day was a special thrill for me. From the day we first met face to face, I had dreamed of flying with Hong My. My dream became a reality as the two of us strapped into my Cessna 172 for the one hour flight to our state capital. After leveling off at 7,000 feet, I asked Hong My, "Do you want to fly it?" And just like any fighter pilot, he immediately adjusted his seat and took the controls. It had been years since Hong My assumed the controls of any aircraft, but he did just fine.

Dan and Hong My airborne in Dan's Cessna 172 enroute to Frankfort, KY, April, 2009.

Our first stop was the beautiful Kentucky Vietnam Veterans Memorial. Hong My was noticeably emotional as the shadow of the memorial's sun dial moved around the granite plaza touching each Kentucky soldier's

name at the exact time he was killed. The memorial's architect, Helm Roberts, was there to meet us and explain the design and symbolism behind the special place. With tears in his eyes, Hong My expressed what was obviously on his heart. "It makes me think about all the soldiers on both sides who were lost and the families they left behind."

On Sunday we attended my church, the State Street United Methodist Church. Quan surprised us all when he remarked, "This is the first time I have ever been in a church." As I witnessed the warmth and acceptance exhibited by my church friends, I paused to give thanks for the freedoms we enjoy in our country.

Kentucky Vietnam Veterans Memorial, Frankfort, KY.

We spent the next day at Western Kentucky University where we participated in a tree planting ceremony to commemorate the visit, a dinner with University President Gary Ransdell, and a special presentation of *My Enemy…My Friend* for the faculty and students.

From Kentucky south to Florida we set our sights on the Sun 'n Fun Fly-In. Hong My and Quan were amazed with all the airplanes, the warm hospitality and celebrity attention. It was during a news conference that I boldly announced, "From this point forward, Hong My, your American nickname is Movie Star." My words must have touched a chord with him as they elicited a huge smile from Hong My and lots of chuckles from the reporters present.

Quan, Syl, Hong My and Dan at church.

We presented our story three times at Sun 'n Fun to the largest crowds they had ever experienced. It was at this

Presentation to Sun 'n Fun crowd at Florida Aviation Museum, April, 2009.

occasion Hong My added to his remarks a request for a "moment of silence" to honor all Vietnam War veterans on both sides. Everyone was moved by his sincerity of friendship and reconciliation, and many of the Vietnam veterans crowded around him for photos after the presentations.

Hong My and Jim Cook in Jim's Yak-9, Lakeland, Fl., April, 2009.

Hong My and I made history in Lakeland, Florida, at Sun 'n Fun, but I knew our most historic opportunities lay ahead. So we were off to Washington D.C., the Smithsonian National Air and Space Museum, and the long awaited reunion with John Stiles.

John and his wife Barbara had arranged to pick us up at the hotel and take us to dinner at a well known Vietnamese restaurant in Arlington. We were seated in the hotel lobby at the appointed time when John walked in. He came directly over to us, greeted me, shook my hand warmly,

John Stiles and Hong My, Washington, D.C., April 26, 2009.

turned to Hong My and said, "I know who you are." The two men grasped each other by the shoulders and just stared at each other for the longest time. There were tears as the two men embraced, and as Steve Hartman of *CBS News* expressed, "the war went away." A new, once unlikely friendship was born that night.

Dinner was highlighted by good conversation. But after dinner John and Hong My, along with the interpreter Phuong Vu, retired to a private table where they had detailed discussions about the day in January 1972, when they first met in mortal combat. I don't know all that was said, but after their conversation John said to me, "Dan, I've been waiting 37 years for this moment. It's as if a huge weight has been lifted off my shoulders. Now I know for sure exactly what happened that day. Hong My told me things only the two of us could know." I felt privileged to have witnessed this remarkable meeting and the completion of the "double full circle."

Events scheduled for the next two days were non-stop. There were visits to the

Hong My and Dan at Vietnam Veterans Memorial.

With Congressman Guthrie (left) and Senator McConnell (right), Washington, D.C., April 2009.

Hong My, Dan and MiG-21 at the Smithsonian National Air and Space Museum, April, 2009.

Smithsonian National Air and Space Museum, the Lincoln Memorial, the Vietnam Veterans Memorial, the White House and the Capitol. We had a private audience with Kentucky's Senator McConnell and Congressman Guthrie, and a little time left-over to prepare for the climax of the whole trip—our presentation for the General Electric Lecture Series in the IMAX Theater at the National Air and Space Museum.

The evening began with a private dinner in the museum hosted by General Richard Daily, the museum director. It was an elegant affair attended by representatives of General Electric and the museum board of directors. After dinner we retired to the theater and began the *My Enemy…*

Dan, Hong My and Phantom 550 at Aviation Heritage Park, Bowling Green, KY, April, 2009.

My Friend presentation. I will long remember that night. What a thrill to observe such a high level of interest in our story and hear the thunderous applause from an audience of over 700 people!

With the applause still resonating in my ears, I close the trunk of the taxi and reluctantly turn to bid farewell to Hong My and his son. Together we express our hope to meet again and to keep our friendship alive, but there is one question left to be answered.

"Movie Star, before you go, will you tell me why you said you didn't like my book, *My Enemy…My Friend*? I really want you to like it."

Hong My answers, "Oh, Anh Dao (my Vietnamese nickname meaning Cherry), I do like your book. I just don't like the title."

"What is wrong with the title?" I ask him.

"Anh Dao, I don't think you and I were ever enemies. We were ***just soldiers*** doing the best we could for our countries during a very difficult time."

I wave good-bye as the taxi pulls away from the curb into the morning traffic. *God speed, my friend,* I utter to myself. *You are right.*

We were. We are, ***Just Soldiers.***

APPENDIX I

McDonnell Douglas F-4D Phantom II

First flown in May 1958, the Phantom II originally was developed for U.S. Navy fleet defense and entered service in 1961. The USAF's Phantom II, designated F-4C, made its first flight on May 27, 1963, and production deliveries began in November 1963. The F-4D was an improved F-4C and made its first flight on December 9, 1965. The F-4D offered an improved bombing and air-to-air capability. The USAF credited F-4D crews with 44 MiG kills over Southeast Asia, more than any other type of aircraft. Phantom II production ended in 1979 after over 5,000 had been built.

The F-4D Phantom II, serial number 66-7550, featured in this story was delivered to the Air Force in March 1967. She flew her last mission in 1989 after accumulating over 6,000 flying hours. Phantom 550 is currently on display at Aviation Heritage Park in Bowling Green, Kentucky.

www.aviationheritagepark.com

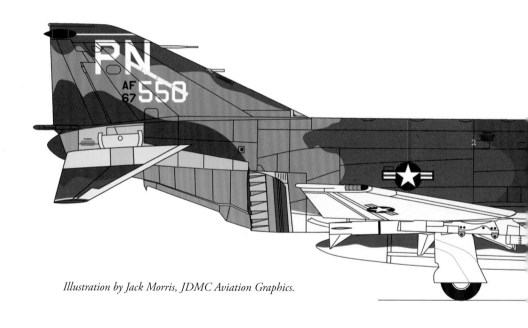

Illustration by Jack Morris, JDMC Aviation Graphics.

SPECIFICATIONS

Span:	38 ft. 5 in.
Length:	58 ft. 2 in.
Height:	16 ft. 6 in.
Weight:	58,000 lbs. loaded

PERFORMANCE

Maximum speed:	1,400 mph
Cruise speed:	590 mph
Range:	1,750 miles
Service ceiling:	59,600 ft.

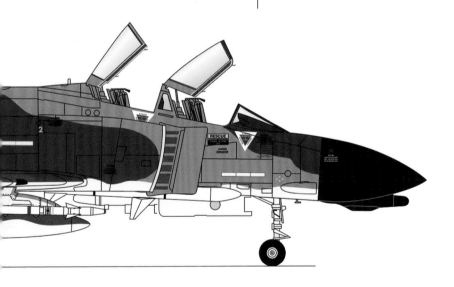

APPENDIX II

Mikoyan-Gurevich MiG-21

The MiG-21 is a single engine, single seat supersonic jet fighter aircraft, designed and built by the Mikoyan-Gurevich Design Bureau in the Soviet Union. The first prototype of the MiG-21 was first flown in 1955 and it made its first public appearance in June 1956. More than 30 countries, including nations friendly to the United States, have flown the MiG-21 and at least 15 versions have been produced. Estimates place the number produced at over 10,000.

In the spring of 1966 the North Vietnamese Air Force (VPAF) began flying the MiG-21. The MiG-21 was one of the most advanced aircraft of the time and it quickly proved to be a worthy opponent of the USAF's F-4 Phantom and F-105 Thunderchief.

Illustration by Jack Morris, JDMC Aviation Graphics.

SPECIFICATIONS

Span:	26 ft. 6 in.
Length:	51 ft. 9 in.
Height:	15 ft. 9 in.
Weight:	18,080 lbs. loaded

PERFORMANCE

Maximum speed:	1,300 mph
Cruise speed:	550 mph
Range:	400 miles
Service ceiling:	50,000 ft.

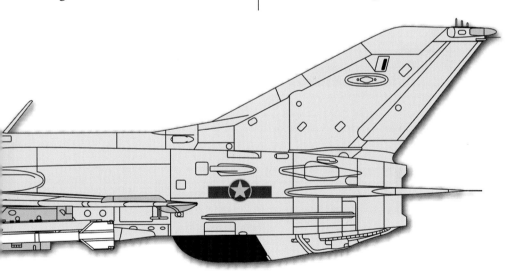

Photographer John Fleck and Dan, Hanoi, Vietnam, April, 2008.

I would like to express my heartfelt thanks to John Fleck for his extraordinary photography. Without John's expertise this story could not be told with the clarity and emotion it deserves. John is a true artist who has contributed his remarkable talent unselfishly. Please take time to review some of John's exceptional work at **www.johnfleck.com**. We are forever grateful, John, for your friendship and dedication to Aviation Heritage Park.

Dan Cherry, October, 2009

ABOUT THE AUTHOR

Edward Daniel "Dan" Cherry is President of Aviation Heritage Park, an educational facility in Bowling Green, Kentucky dedicated to inspiring the youth of today by exhibiting aviation artifacts that represent the stories and careers of distinguished aviators from South Central Kentucky. He recently retired as President of the Kentucky Transpark, a large economic development project for south central Kentucky. Dan stays very active in community and state affairs serving on numerous boards and commissions.

Dan developed his leadership skills during his career as a fighter pilot in the United States Air Force. He entered the Air Force in 1959 as an Aviation Cadet and was commissioned a Second Lieutenant in 1960. His military credentials include flying 295 combat missions during the Vietnam War and shooting down a North Vietnamese MiG-21. He held the positions of Commander and Leader of the Air Force Thunderbirds; Commander of Moody Air Force Base, Georgia; Inspector General of the Pacific Air Forces; Commander of the 8th Tactical Fighter Wing and Commander of the Air Force Recruiting Service. He earned several military awards and decorations including the Distinguished Service Medal, the Silver Star with one oak leaf cluster, the Legion of Merit with two oak leaf clusters, the Distinguished Flying Cross with nine oak leaf clusters and the Air Medal with thirty four oak leaf clusters. He completed his service in the Air Force with the rank of Brigadier General. Dan has also served in Kentucky state government as Secretary of the Kentucky Justice Cabinet. He was inducted into the Kentucky Aviation Hall of Fame in October 2000.